Seraphim and Cherubim

A Scriptural Chaplet of the Holy Angels

By Christine Haapala

Suffering Servant Scriptorium
Fairfax, VA
www.sufferingservant.com

Published with Ecclesiastical Permission
Diocese of Arlington
November 17, 2010

Scripture excerpts from the *New American Bible with Revised New Testament and Psalms* Copyright © 1991, 1986, 1970 by the Confraternity of Christian Doctrine, Washington, D.C. Used with permission. All Rights Reserved. No part of the *New American Bible* may be reproduced in any form without permission in writing from the copyright owner.

Illustrations on pages: Cover, iii, vi, viii, 1, 5, 11, 16, 22, 24, 27, 28, 30, 31 are from "Angels" by Alan Weller, © Dover Publications, Inc., July, 2009
Illustrations on pages: 7, 9, 12, 17, 18, 19, 21 are from "120 Great Paintings of the Life of Jesus," ed. Carol Belanger Grafton © Dover Publications, Inc., September, 2008
Illustrations on pages: 2, 4, 6, 14, 32 are from "120 Italian Renaissance Paintings," ed. Carol Belanger Grafton © Dover Publications, Inc., December, 2007

Dover Publications, Inc., 31 East Second Street, Mineola, NY 11501
www.doverpublications.com

Used with permission.

Cover design and layout by Alison Ujueta

Copyright © 2010, Christine Haapala
All Rights Reserved.

ISBN 978-0-9703996-1-8

Manufactured in the United States of America.

Dedicated to Blessed Mary ever Virgin,
Queen of Angels

Special thanks to Father Michael Duesterhaus for all his
encouragement and spiritual direction.

Table of Illustrations

Detail; *The Wilton Diptych*; c. 1395-9	Cover
The Coronation of the Virgin; JAN BAEGERT, 16th c.	iii
The Annunciation; LORENZO MONACO, c. 1410-15	vi
The Fall of the Rebel Angels; PIETER BRUEGEL THE ELDER, 1562	viii
St. Michael	1
Expulsion from Paradise; GIOVANNI DI PAOLO, 1445	2
The Sacrifice of Isaac; ANDREA DEL SARTO, c. 1528-29	4
Jacob's Dream; SCHOOL OF PROVENCE, 15th c.	5
Archangel Raphael with Tobias; PIETRO PERUGINO, c. 1496-1500	6
Annunciation; HANS MEMLING, 1482	7
The Annunciation to the Shepherds; BOUCICAUT MASTER, c. 1405-8	9
The Adoration of the Shepherds; ANTON RAFAEL MENGS, 1779	11
The Temptation of Christ on the Mountain; DUCCIO DI BUONINSEGNA, 1308-11	12
The Agony in the Garden; ANDREA MANTEGNA, c. 1460	14
The Trinity with Christ Crucified; AUSTRIAN SCHOOL, c. 1410	16
The Resurrection of Christ; RAPHAEL, 1499-1502	17
The Three Marys at the Tomb; ADOLPHONE WILLIAM BOUGUEREAU, c. 1900	18
From *The Ascension*; ANDREA MANTEGNA, 1462	19
Christ Giving the Blessing; FERNANDO GALLEGO, c. 1492	21
The Last Judgment altarpiece; VAN DER WEYDEN, 1445-1450	22
From *The Bamberg Apocalypse*; 15th c.	24
The Celestial Army; GUARIENTO DI ARPO, 1378	27
Seraphim with Six Wings; 12th/13th c.	28
Angels Holding Scrolls; c. 1450	30
From *The Coronation of the Virgin*; RIDOLFO GHIRLANDAIO, 1504	31
Angels; BENOZZO GOZZOLI, c. 1459	32

Table of Contents

Table of Illustrations	iv
Rosaries or Chaplets? Just Pray Always	vii
The Chaplet of the Holy Angels	1
First Angelic Decade: Angels of Adam, Abraham, and Moses	3
Second Angelic Decade: Angels of the Child Jesus, Our Lord and Savior	7
Third Angelic Decade: Angels of the Messiah, Jesus Crucified	13
Fourth Angelic Decade: Angels of the Risen Christ	17
Fifth Angelic Decade: Angels at the End of the Age	23
Novena of the Holy Angels	29
Litany of the Holy Angels	33

Rosaries or Chaplets? Just Pray Always.

We know that angels are God's messengers, but to truly understand them we need to see the word angel as more verb than noun. Angels are always 'messenging' - they are always in the presence of God and yet, in the case of our Guardian Angels, are at the same time, by our sides here on earth.

This conduit to eternity, this spiritual link of heaven to earth, this bond between God and man is one of the most over-looked assets in our modern world. Angels are creatures with a will and an intellect. They can be wonderful partners in prayer, but only if we call upon them.

Anyone familiar with the writings of the great saints, from St. Theresa to St. Ignatius of Loyola, has read the phrase, "spiritual exercises." These steps of reading, meditation, mortification, and prayer can take numerous formats, but always have the same purpose: drawing us closer to our Lord and God.

Focusing on the term 'exercises' for a moment, what physical exercise does for the body, spiritual exercise does for our soul. The more you exercise, the stronger you are - and it is in steady, regular prayer that we will grow in the strength of God's grace.

See in this wonderful chaplet not a replacement for your current life of prayer, but rather a complimentary addition. Again, exercise of the body involves all sorts of activities: running, lifting, and pushing. Our prayer life should have a whole spectrum of activities so that we develop in all sorts of ways. See this chaplet not as a replacement of the rosary, but rather, another way to grow in love for Our Lord.

Fr. Michael R. Duesterhaus
Diocese of Arlington

Our Lady of Angels Catholic Church
Woodbridge, Virginia

The Chaplet of the Holy Angels

Open the chaplet with the *Sign of the Cross* and the *Prayer to Saint Michael*. On the Our Father beads of a rosary, say the *Prayer to your Guardian Angel*. On the decade of ten Hail Mary beads of a rosary, pray the ten Sacred Scripture verses with the short invocation requesting the prayers of Our Lady, Queen of Angels, and Archangels Michael, Gabriel, and Raphael. Pause briefly after each Scripture verse and reflect on the Word of God. Follow each decade of Sacred Scripture verses with a *Glory Be*. Conclude the chaplet with the *Prayer to Saint Michael* and the *Sign of the Cross*.

In the name of the Father, and of the Son, and of the Holy Spirit. Amen.

Saint Michael the Archangel, defend us in battle. Be our protection against the wickedness and snares of the devil. May God rebuke him, we humbly pray; and do Thou, O Prince of the Heavenly Host by the Divine Power of God cast into hell, Satan and all the evil spirits, who roam throughout the world seeking the ruin of souls. Amen.

First Angelic Decade
Angels of Adam, Abraham, and Moses

Angel of God, My Guardian Dear to whom God's love commits me here.
Ever this day be at my side to light and guard and rule and guide. Amen.

The LORD God therefore banished him from the garden of Eden … [and] settled him east of the garden of Eden; and he stationed the cherubim and the fiery revolving sword, to guard the way to the tree of life. … "He makes his angels winds / and his ministers a fiery flame." *Gn 3:23-24, Heb 1:7*

Our Lady, Queen of Angels, pray for us.
Michael, Gabriel, and Raphael, holy Archangels, pray for us.

[T]he angels said to Lot: … "We are about to destroy this place, for the outcry reaching the LORD against those in the city is so great that he has sent us to destroy it." … As he looked down toward Sodom and Gomorrah, … he saw dense smoke over the land rising like fumes from a furnace. *Gn 19:12-13,28*

Our Lady, Queen of Angels, pray for us.
Michael, Gabriel, and Raphael, holy Archangels, pray for us.

Abraham built an altar there and arranged the wood on it. … But the LORD's messenger called to him from heaven, "Abraham, Abraham! … I know now how devoted you are to God, since you did not withhold from me your beloved son." *Gn 22:9, 11-12*

Our Lady, Queen of Angels, pray for us.
Michael, Gabriel, and Raphael, holy Archangels, pray for us.

Again the LORD's messenger called to Abraham from heaven … "I will bless you abundantly and make your descendants as countless as the stars of the sky and the sands of the seashore." *Gn 22:15,17*

Our Lady, Queen of Angels, pray for us.
Michael, Gabriel, and Raphael, holy Archangels, pray for us.

[Jacob] had a dream: a stairway ... reaching to the heavens; and God's messengers were going up and down on it. And there was the LORD standing beside him and saying: "I, the LORD, am the God of your forefather Abraham and the God of Isaac ..." *Gen 28:12-13*

> *Our Lady, Queen of Angels, pray for us.*
> *Michael, Gabriel, and Raphael,*
> *holy Archangels, pray for us.*

Horeb, the mountain of God. There an angel of the LORD appeared to [Moses] in fire flaming out of a bush. ... [T]he LORD said, "I have witnessed the affliction of my people and have heard their cry. ... I will send you to Pharaoh to lead my people, the Israelites, out of Egypt." *Ex 3:1-2,7,10*

> *Our Lady, Queen of Angels, pray for us.*
> *Michael, Gabriel, and Raphael,*
> *holy Archangels, pray for us.*

"See, I am sending an angel before you, to guard you on the way and bring you to the place I have prepared. Be attentive to him and heed his voice." ... The LORD told Moses, ... "I will send an angel before you to the land flowing with milk and honey." *Ex 23:20-21; 33:1-2*

Our Lady, Queen of Angels, pray for us.
Michael, Gabriel, and Raphael, holy Archangels, pray for us.

"I am Raphael, one of the seven angels who enter and serve before the Glory of the Lord." ... They kept thanking God and singing his praises; and they continued to acknowledge these marvelous deeds which he had done when the angel of the Lord appeared to them. *Tobit 12:15,22*

Our Lady, Queen of Angels, pray for us.
Michael, Gabriel, and Raphael, holy Archangels, pray for us.

The priests brought the ark of the covenant of the LORD to its place beneath the wings of the cherubim in the sanctuary, the holy of holies of the temple. The cherubim had their wings spread out over the place of the ark, sheltering the ark. ... There was nothing in it but the two tablets which Moses put there on Horeb. *2 Chr 5:7-8,10*

Our Lady, Queen of Angels, pray for us.
Michael, Gabriel, and Raphael, holy Archangels, pray for us.

From your throne upon the cherubim reveal yourself … / Stir up your power, come to save us. / O LORD of hosts, restore us. *Ps 80:2-4*

Our Lady, Queen of Angels, pray for us.
Michael, Gabriel, and Raphael, holy Archangels, pray for us.

Glory be to the Father…

SECOND ANGELIC DECADE
ANGELS OF THE CHILD JESUS, OUR LORD AND SAVIOR

Angel of God, My Guardian Dear to whom God's love commits me here.
Ever this day be at my side to light and guard and rule and guide. Amen.

[T]he angel of the Lord appeared to him, standing at the right of the altar of incense. … [T]he angel said to him, "Do not be afraid, Zechariah, because your prayer has been heard. Your wife Elizabeth will bear you a son, and you shall name him John." *Lk 1:11,13*

Our Lady, Queen of Angels,
pray for us.
Michael, Gabriel, and Raphael,
holy Archangels, pray for us.

[T]he angel Gabriel was sent from God to a town of Galilee called Nazareth, to a virgin … Mary. *Lk 1:26-27*

Our Lady, Queen of Angels,
pray for us.
Michael, Gabriel, and Raphael,
holy Archangels, pray for us.

Then the angel said to her, ... "Behold, you will conceive in your womb and bear a son, and you shall name him Jesus." ... Praise the LORD from the heavens; / ... Praise him, all you angels; / give praise, all you hosts. *Lk 1:30-31, Ps 148:1-2*

> *Our Lady, Queen of Angels, pray for us.*
> *Michael, Gabriel, and Raphael, holy Archangels, pray for us.*

And the angel said ... "The holy Spirit will come upon you, and the power of the Most High will overshadow you. Therefore the child to be born will be called holy, the Son of God." *Lk 1:35*

> *Our Lady, Queen of Angels, pray for us.*
> *Michael, Gabriel, and Raphael, holy Archangels, pray for us.*

[B]ehold, the angel of the Lord appeared to him in a dream and said, "Joseph, son of David, do not be afraid to take Mary your wife into your home. For it is through the holy Spirit that this child has been conceived in her." *Mt 1:20*

> *Our Lady, Queen of Angels, pray for us.*
> *Michael, Gabriel, and Raphael, holy Archangels, pray for us.*

The angel of the Lord appeared to [the shepherds] and the glory of the Lord shone around them. ... The angel said to them, "Do not be afraid; for behold, I proclaim to you good news of great joy. ... [A] savior has been born for you who is Messiah and Lord." *Lk 2:9-11*

> *Our Lady, Queen of Angels, pray for us.*
> *Michael, Gabriel, and Raphael, holy Archangels, pray for us.*

And suddenly there was a multitude of the heavenly host with the angel, praising God and saying: / "Glory to God in the highest." *Lk 2:13-14*

Our Lady, Queen of Angels, pray for us.
Michael, Gabriel, and Raphael, holy Archangels, pray for us.

"Angels of the Lord, bless the Lord, / praise and exalt him above all forever." ... "Let all the angels of God worship him." *Dan 3:58, Heb 1:6*

Our Lady, Queen of Angels, pray for us.
Michael, Gabriel, and Raphael, holy Archangels, pray for us.

[B]ehold, the angel of the Lord appeared to Joseph in a dream and said, "Rise, take the child and his mother, flee to Egypt, and stay there until I tell you. Herod is going to search for the child to destroy him." *Mt 2:13*

Our Lady, Queen of Angels, pray for us.
Michael, Gabriel, and Raphael, holy Archangels, pray for us.

[B]ehold, the angel of the Lord appeared to Joseph in a dream in Egypt and said, "Rise, take the child and his mother and go to the land of Israel, for those who sought the child's life are dead." *Mt 2:19-20*

Our Lady, Queen of Angels, pray for us.
Michael, Gabriel, and Raphael, holy Archangels, pray for us.

Glory be to the Father…

Third Angelic Decade
Angels of the Messiah, Jesus Crucified

Angel of God, My Guardian Dear to whom God's love commits me here.
Ever this day be at my side to light and guard and rule and guide. Amen.

Are [the angels] not all ministering spirits sent to serve, for the sake of those who are to inherit salvation? *Heb 1:14*

Our Lady, Queen of Angels, pray for us.
Michael, Gabriel, and Raphael, holy Archangels, pray for us.

Michael and his angels battled against the dragon. The dragon and its angels fought back, but they did not prevail and there was no longer any place for them in heaven. *Rv 12:7-8*

Our Lady, Queen of Angels, pray for us.
Michael, Gabriel, and Raphael, holy Archangels, pray for us.

[Jesus] remained in the desert for forty days, tempted by Satan. He was among wild beasts, and the angels ministered to him. ... Thousands upon thousands were ministering to him, / and myriads upon myriads attended him. *Mk 1:13, Dn 7:10*

Our Lady, Queen of Angels, pray for us.
Michael, Gabriel, and Raphael, holy Archangels, pray for us.

For God commands the angels / to guard you in all your ways. ... / lest you strike your foot against a stone. *Ps 91:11-12*

Our Lady, Queen of Angels, pray for us.
Michael, Gabriel, and Raphael, holy Archangels, pray for us.

And he spoke to them at length in parables, saying: … "He who sows good seed is the Son of Man, the field is the world, the good seed the children of the kingdom. The weeds are the children of the evil one, and the enemy who sows them is the devil. The harvest is the end of the age, and the harvesters are angels." *Mt 13:3,37-39*

Our Lady, Queen of Angels, pray for us.
Michael, Gabriel, and Raphael, holy Archangels, pray for us.

[And to strengthen him an angel from heaven appeared to him. He was in such agony and he prayed so fervently that his sweat became like drops of blood falling on the ground.] *Lk 22:43-44*

Our Lady, Queen of Angels, pray for us.
Michael, Gabriel, and Raphael, holy Archangels, pray for us.

"Do you think that I cannot call upon my Father and he will provide me at this moment with more than twelve legions of angels?" *Mt 26:53*

Our Lady, Queen of Angels, pray for us.
Michael, Gabriel, and Raphael, holy Archangels, pray for us.

Bless the LORD, all you angels, / mighty in strength and attentive, / obedient to every command. *Ps 103:20*

Our Lady, Queen of Angels, pray for us.
Michael, Gabriel, and Raphael, holy Archangels, pray for us.

When they came to the place called the Skull, they crucified him and the criminals. ... Then [the criminal] said, "Jesus, remember me when you come into your kingdom." ... "I tell you, there will be rejoicing among the angels of God over one sinner who repents." *Lk 23:33,42; 15:10*

Our Lady, Queen of Angels, pray for us.
Michael, Gabriel, and Raphael, holy Archangels, pray for us.

I ... heard the voices of many angels who surrounded the throne ... and they cried out in a loud voice: / "Worthy is the Lamb that was slain / to receive power and riches, wisdom and strength, / honor and glory and blessing." *Rv 5:11-12*

Our Lady, Queen of Angels, pray for us.
Michael, Gabriel, and Raphael, holy Archangels, pray for us.

Glory be to the Father...

Fourth Angelic Decade
Angels of the Risen Christ

Angel of God, My Guardian Dear to whom God's love commits me here.
Ever this day be at my side to light and guard and rule and guide. Amen.

The LORD is king … / God is enthroned on the cherubim. *Ps 99:1*

Our Lady, Queen of Angels, pray for us.
Michael, Gabriel, and Raphael, holy Archangels, pray for us.

And behold, there was a great earthquake; for an angel of the Lord descended from heaven, approached, rolled back the stone and sat upon it. *Mt 28:2*

Our Lady, Queen of Angels, pray for us. Michael, Gabriel, and Raphael, holy Archangels, pray for us.

Mary ... bent over into the tomb and saw two angels in white sitting there, one at the head and one at the feet where the body of Jesus had been. *Jn 20:11-12*

Our Lady, Queen of Angels, pray for us.
Michael, Gabriel, and Raphael, holy Archangels, pray for us.

Then the angel said to the women ... "Do not be afraid! I know that you are seeking Jesus the crucified. He is not here, for he has been raised just as he said." *Mt 28:5-6*

Our Lady, Queen of Angels,
pray for us.
Michael, Gabriel, and Raphael,
holy Archangels, pray for us.

Some women ... were at the tomb early in the morning and did not find his body; they came back and reported that they had indeed seen a vision of angels who announced that he was alive. *Lk 24:22-23*

Our Lady, Queen of Angels,
pray for us.
Michael, Gabriel, and Raphael,
holy Archangels, pray for us.

"Amen, amen, I say to you, you will see the sky opened and the angels of God ascending and descending on the Son of Man." *Jn 1:51*

Our Lady, Queen of Angels, pray for us.
Michael, Gabriel, and Raphael, holy Archangels, pray for us.

[S]uddenly two men dressed in white garments ... said, "Men of Galilee, why are you standing there looking at the sky? This Jesus who has been taken up from you into heaven will return in the same way you have seen him going into heaven." *Acts 1:10-11*

> *Our Lady, Queen of Angels, pray for us.*
> *Michael, Gabriel, and Raphael, holy Archangels, pray for us.*

When he had accomplished purification from sins, / he took his seat at the right hand of the Majesty on high, / as far superior to the angels... *Heb 1:3-4*

> *Our Lady, Queen of Angels, pray for us.*
> *Michael, Gabriel, and Raphael, holy Archangels, pray for us.*

I saw the Lord seated on a high and lofty throne. ... Seraphim were stationed above; each of them had six wings. ... "Holy, holy, holy is the LORD of hosts!" they cried one to the other. *Is 6:1-3*

> *Our Lady, Queen of Angels, pray for us.*
> *Michael, Gabriel, and Raphael, holy Archangels, pray for us.*

All the angels stood around the throne. ... They prostrated themselves before the throne, worshipped God, and exclaimed: / "Amen. Blessing and glory, wisdom and thanksgiving, / honor, power, and might / be to our God forever and ever. Amen." *Rv 7:11-12*

> *Our Lady, Queen of Angels, pray for us.*
> *Michael, Gabriel, and Raphael, holy Archangels, pray for us.*

> *Glory be to the Father...*

Fifth Angelic Decade
Angels at the End of the Age

Angel of God, My Guardian Dear to whom God's love commits me here.
Ever this day be at my side to light and guard and rule and guide. Amen.

"Just as weeds are collected and burned [up] with fire, so it will be at the end of the age. The Son of Man will send his angels, and they will collect out of his kingdom all those who cause others to sin and all evildoers. They will throw them into the fiery furnace." *Mt 13:40-42*

Our Lady, Queen of Angels, pray for us.
Michael, Gabriel, and Raphael, holy Archangels, pray for us.

"When the Son of Man comes in his glory, and all the angels with him, he will sit upon his glorious throne, and all the nations will be assembled before him. And he will separate them one from another, as a shepherd separates the sheep from the goats." *Mt 25:31-32*

Our Lady, Queen of Angels, pray for us.
Michael, Gabriel, and Raphael, holy Archangels, pray for us.

I saw four angels standing at the four corners of the earth, holding back the four winds. … [The angel] cried out in a loud voice to the four angels, … "Do not damage the land or the sea or the trees until we put the seal on the foreheads of the servants of our God." *Rv 7:1-3*

Our Lady, Queen of Angels, pray for us.
Michael, Gabriel, and Raphael, holy Archangels, pray for us.

I saw that the seven angels who stood before God were given seven trumpets. ... When the first one blew his trumpet, there came hail and fire mixed with blood. ... [A] large burning mountain was hurled into the sea. ... [A] large star burning like a torch fell from the sky. ... [T]he day lost its light for a third of the time. ... [L]ocusts came out of the smoke onto the land. ... By these three plagues of fire, smoke, and sulphur ... a third of the human race was killed.
Rv 8:2,7,8,10,12; 9:3,18

Our Lady, Queen of Angels,
pray for us.
Michael, Gabriel,
and Raphael,
holy Archangels,
pray for us.

Then the seventh angel blew his trumpet. ... God's temple in heaven was opened, and the ark of the covenant could be seen in the temple. There were flashes of lightning... *Rv 11:15,19*

Our Lady, Queen of Angels, pray for us.
Michael, Gabriel, and Raphael, holy Archangels, pray for us.

"[T]hey will see the Son of Man coming upon the clouds of heaven with power and great glory. And he will send out his angels with a trumpet blast, and they will gather his elect from the four winds." ... "For the Son of Man will come with his angels in his Father's glory, and then he will repay everyone according to his conduct." *Mt 24:30-31, Mt 16:27*

Our Lady, Queen of Angels, pray for us.
Michael, Gabriel, and Raphael, holy Archangels, pray for us.

I saw another angel flying high overhead, with everlasting good news to those who dwell on earth ... "Fear God and give him glory, for his time has come to sit in judgment. Worship him who made heaven and earth..." *Rv 14:6-7*

Our Lady, Queen of Angels, pray for us.
Michael, Gabriel, and Raphael, holy Archangels, pray for us.

I heard a loud voice speaking from the temple to the seven angels, "Go and pour out the seven bowls of God's fury upon the earth." ... festering and ugly sores ... sea turned to blood ... rivers ... turned to blood ... scorching heat ... darkness ... water was dried up ... a great earthquake. *Rv 16:1-4,9-10,12,18*

Our Lady, Queen of Angels, pray for us.
Michael, Gabriel, and Raphael, holy Archangels, pray for us.

Then I saw an angel come down from heaven, holding in his hand the key to the abyss and a heavy chain. He seized the dragon … and tied it up for a thousand years and threw it into the abyss … so that it could no longer lead the nations astray. *Rv 20:1-3*

Our Lady, Queen of Angels, pray for us.
Michael, Gabriel, and Raphael, holy Archangels, pray for us.

The seven angels with the seven plagues came out of the temple. … "But of that day and hour no one knows, neither the angels of heaven, nor the Son, but the Father alone." *Rv 15:6; Mt 24:36*

Our Lady, Queen of Angels, pray for us.
Michael, Gabriel, and Raphael, holy Archangels, pray for us.

Glory be to the Father…

Saint Michael the Archangel, defend us in battle. Be our protection against the wickedness and snares of the devil. May God rebuke him, we humbly pray; and do Thou, O Prince of the Heavenly Host by the Divine Power of God cast into hell, Satan and all the evil spirits, who roam throughout the world seeking the ruin of souls. Amen.

In the name of the Father, and of the Son, and of the Holy Spirit. Amen.

Novena of the Holy Angels

> Begin with these introductory prayers, then pray the Chaplet of the Holy Angels that starts on page 1. Pray this sequence for nine consecutive days. Begin the nine days on a special day, such as, the Feast of the Archangels, September 29th, the Feast of the Guardian Angels, October 2nd, your birthday, or any day you wish special protection and favors from the angels.
>
> Additionally, you could pray this novena for nine consecutive hours, beginning at 7 a.m. and concluding at the ninth hour, 3 p.m., the Hour of Mercy.
>
> *And when the sixth hour was come, there was darkness over the whole earth until the ninth hour. And at the ninth hour, Jesus cried with a loud voice ... My God, my God, why hast thou forsaken me? ... And Jesus having cried out with a loud voice, gave up the ghost.* Mk 15:33-34,37 (DR)

Let us pray these nine days (or nine hours).

Archangel Michael, Prince of Angels, who cast the demonic dragon out of heaven, shield us from Satan's deceit, as you protected Jesus on the mountaintop. Together with your angelic army, help us navigate around the turbulent temptations of the world. Be ever vigilant in our protection, in the safeguard of our loved ones, and in the shelter of those of the whole world. Teach us true contrition for all our faults and failings.

Seraphim, adoring at the Celestial Tabernacle, join us at the Eucharistic Table and envelop us with the love of Jesus Christ. Instruct us in the ways to unreservedly adore Our Lord in His Holy and Real Presence. Cherubim, immersed in the Beatific Vision, direct us toward our Heavenly Home to adore the Triune God for all eternity.

Angels of the Hallelujah Chorus, giving praise in song and thunderous trumpet blasts, elevate our heart and mind to adore the Giver of Life. Let us thank Him for everything, both great and small.

Angels of the Heavenly Host, we are most unworthy to ask this favor. On our behalf, please graciously carry this appeal _____ to the throne of your Heavenly Queen. Pray with us that Mary Most Holy, Queen of Angels, presents this request to her Son. If it is His will, may He grant this yearning we ardently pray for today.

Litany of the Holy Angels

> A litany is a responsive form of petition prayer. Only a few litanies are approved for public liturgical services, such as, The Litany to the Sacred Heart. This Litany of the Holy Angels is to be prayed during private devotions. An example of a private devotion is a small prayer group that meets weekly to pray for a particular request, like the end of abortion.
>
> In praying a litany, in chorus fashion, the prayer leader requests the assistance of Our Lord, Our Lady, or a saint, and then the prayer group responds with the petitions, such as, have mercy on us or pray for us. This angelic litany is part of the sacred tradition of Catholic prayer, author unknown.

Lord, have mercy.	*Lord, have mercy.*
Christ, have mercy.	*Christ, have mercy.*
Lord, have mercy.	*Lord, have mercy.*
Christ, hear us.	*Christ, graciously hear us.*
God, the Father of Heaven,	*have mercy on us.*
God, the Son, Redeemer of the world,	*have mercy on us.*
God, the Holy Ghost,	*have mercy on us.*
Holy Trinity, One God,	*have mercy on us.*
Holy Mary, Queen of Angels,	*pray for us.*
Holy Mother of God,	*pray for us.*
Holy Virgin of virgins,	*pray for us.*

Saint Michael,
  who was ever the defender of the people of God, *pray for us.*
Saint Michael,
  who did drive from Heaven Lucifer and his rebel crew, *pray for us.*
Saint Michael,
  who did cast down to Hell the accuser of our brethren, *pray for us.*
Saint Gabriel,
  who did expound to Daniel the heavenly vision, *pray for us.*
Saint Gabriel,
  who did foretell to Zachary the birth and ministry of John the Baptist, *pray for us.*
Saint Gabriel,
  who did announce to Blessed Mary the Incarnation of the Divine Word, *pray for us.*
Saint Raphael,
  who did lead Tobias safely through his journey to his home again, *pray for us.*
Saint Raphael,
  who did deliver Sara from the devil, *pray for us.*
Saint Raphael,
  who did restore his sight to Tobias the elder, *pray for us.*

All ye holy Angels, who stand around the high and lofty throne of God, *pray for us.*
Who cry to Him continually: Holy, Holy, Holy, *pray for us.*
Who dispel the darkness of our minds and give us light, *pray for us.*
Who are the messengers of heavenly things to men, *pray for us.*
Who have been appointed by God to be our guardians, *pray for us.*
Who always behold the Face of our Father Who is in Heaven, *pray for us.*
Who rejoice over one sinner doing penance, *pray for us.*
Who struck the Sodomites with blindness, *pray for us.*

Who led Lot out of the midst of the ungodly, *pray for us.*
Who ascended and descended on the ladder of Jacob, *pray for us.*
Who delivered the Divine Law to Moses on Mount Sinai, *pray for us.*
Who brought good tidings when Christ was born, *pray for us.*
Who comforted Him in His agony, *pray for us.*
Who sat in white garments at His sepulcher, *pray for us.*
Who appeared to the disciples as He went up into Heaven, *pray for us.*
Who shall go before Him bearing the standard of the Cross
  when He comes to judgment, *pray for us.*
Who shall gather together the elect at the End of the World, *pray for us.*
Who shall separate the wicked from among the just, *pray for us.*
Who offer to God the prayers of those who pray, *pray for us.*
Who assist us at the hour of death, *pray for us.*
Who carried Lazarus into Abraham's bosom, *pray for us.*
Who conduct to Heaven the souls of the just, *pray for us.*
Who perform signs and wonders by the power of God, *pray for us.*
Who are sent to minister for those who shall receive
  the inheritance of salvation, *pray for us.*
Who are set over kingdoms and provinces, *pray for us.*
Who have often put to flight armies of enemies, *pray for us.*
Who have often delivered God's servants from prison
  and other perils of this life, *pray for us.*
Who have often consoled the holy martyrs in their torments, *pray for us.*
Who are wont to cherish with peculiar care the
  prelates and princes of the Church, *pray for us.*
All ye holy orders of blessed spirits, *pray for us.*

From all dangers,	*deliver us, O Lord.*
From the snares of the devil,	*deliver us, O Lord.*
From all heresy and schism,	*deliver us, O Lord.*
From plague, famine and wars,	*deliver us, O Lord.*
From sudden and unlooked-for death,	*deliver us, O Lord.*
From everlasting death,	*deliver us, O Lord.*
Through Thy holy Angels,	*we beseech Thee, hear us.*
That Thou would spare us,	*we beseech Thee, hear us.*
That Thou would pardon us,	*we beseech Thee, hear us.*
That Thou would govern and preserve Thy Holy Church,	*we beseech Thee, hear us.*
That Thou would protect our Apostolic Prelate and all ecclesiastical orders,	*we beseech Thee, hear us.*
That Thou would grant peace and security to kings and all Christian princes,	*we beseech Thee, hear us.*
That Thou would give and preserve the fruits of the earth,	*we beseech Thee, hear us.*
That Thou would grant eternal rest to all the faithful departed,	*we beseech Thee, hear us.*
Lamb of God, Who takes away the sins of the world,	*spare us, O Lord.*
Lamb of God, Who takes away the sins of the world,	*graciously hear us, O Lord.*
Lamb of God, Who takes away the sins of the world,	*have mercy on us.*
Lord, have mercy.	*Christ, have mercy.*
Lord, have mercy.	

Our Father ... Hail Mary ... Glory Be

Bless the Lord, all ye Angels, *ye who are mighty in strength, who fulfill His commandments, hearkening unto the voice of His words.*

He hath given His Angels charge concerning thee, *to keep thee in all thy ways.*

Let Us Pray.

O God, Who dost arrange the services of Angels and men in a wonderful order, mercifully grant that our life may be protected on earth by those who always do Thee service in Heaven, through Jesus Christ Thy Son, Who with Thee and the Holy Ghost are one God now and forever.

Amen.

O God, Who in Thine unspeakable Providence dost send Thine Angels to keep guard over us, grant unto Thy suppliants that we may be continually defended by their protection and may rejoice eternally in their society, through Jesus Christ Our Lord, Who lives and reigns with Thee, in the unity of the Holy Ghost, forever and ever.

Amen.

Other Titles available from Suffering Servant Scriptorium

Prayer Books for Children of All Ages

Speak, Lord, I am Listening A Rosary Book (2nd Ed, with Luminous Mysteries. Includes Study and Discussion Guide) This prayer book presents the richness of the Sacred Mysteries of the Most Holy Rosary in terms that children can visualize and understand. Gus Muller's watercolors use the full palette of color expression to explore the depths of the agony of Christ crucified and reach the heights of the Blessed Virgin Mary's glorious reign as Queen of Heaven and Earth. Succinct and most apt meditation selections yield a wealth of spiritual insight into the mysterious events of the lives of Jesus and Mary. The Scriptures and watercolor illustrations coupled with the prayers of the Most Holy Rosary provide a rich meditation platform for teaching prayer and devotion to Jesus and Mary.

Follow Me A Stations of the Cross Book. Inspired watercolors and selections of God's Word introduce children to the suffering of our Savior Jesus Christ by walking each step with Him to Calvary. Along with each station is a heroically holy person who epitomized self-sacrifice and was beatified or canonized by Pope John Paul II.

Prayer Books for Adults and Teenagers

In His Presence: Seven Visits to the Blessed Sacrament This meditation book outlines SEVEN VISITS to the Blessed Sacrament. This prayer book can be used in one evening, such as, during the Holy Thursday Seven Church Pilgrimage. It can be used for seven consecutive days for a special prayer request. And, it can be used periodically, whenever you can spend time visiting Jesus in the Blessed Sacrament.

 <u>Psalter of Jesus and Mary</u> This pocket-size Scriptural Rosary prayer book includes the 150 Psalms Scriptural Rosary for the Joyful, Sorrowful and Glorious Mysteries and meditations for the Luminous Mysteries from the Book of Proverbs, the wise words of Solomon. The 20 Mysteries of the Most Holy Rosary open with a New Testament reflection. There is a short Scripture meditation from either Psalms or Proverbs for each Hail Mary. An Old and New Testament icon from Julius Schnorr von Carolsfeld's <u>Treasurey of Bible Illustrations</u> accompany each mystery.

 <u>His Sorrowful Passion</u> This prayer book integrates Sacred Scripture meditations with the prayers of the Chaplet of Divine Mercy. There are two Scriptural Chaplets: one chronicles Jesus' Passion and the other features the Seven Penitential Psalms. The woodcuts of the 15th century Catholic artist, Albrecht Durer, illustrate this book.

 <u>The Suffering Servant's Courage</u> (2nd Ed, with Luminous Mysteries) This prayer book integrates poignant Sacred Scripture verses about courage and fortitude, the prayers of the Most Holy Rosary, and illustrations from the inspired artistry of the 19th century Catholic illustrator Gustave Dore.

 <u>From Genesis to Revelation: Seven Scriptural Rosaries</u> This prayer book is the most thorough and extensive collection of Scriptural Rosaries you will find anywhere. This prayer book goes well beyond the traditional Scriptural Rosary and penetrates the heart of the meditative spirit of the mysteries. It addresses many dimensions: time, from the Old to the New Testament; authors, from Moses, Isaiah, to the Evangelists; and perspectives, form the purely historical to deeper spiritual and prayerful insights. Those who pray the Rosary and those who read the Bible will equally find this prayer book inspirational.

Recorded Prayers available on CD

The Sanctity of Life Scriptural Rosary (2nd Ed. with Luminous Mysteries) Sacred Scripture selections prayed with the Most Holy Rosary uniquely brings you God's message of the dignity and sanctity of life. The prayers are accompanied by meditative piano music. Four different readers lead you in more than two hours of prayerful meditations. Includes four songs from the composer and soprano Nancy Scimone, winner of the UNITY Awards 2002 Best Sacramental Album of the Year for ORA PRO NOBIS. Includes 16-page book with the complete text of the Sacred Scripture selections. Double CD. CD 1 includes the Joyful and Luminous Mysteries and CD 2 includes the Sorrowful and Glorious Mysteries.

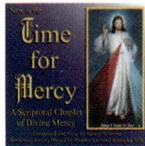

Time for Mercy Composer and singer Nancy Scimone offers you a new, spiritually uplifting Chaplet of Divine Mercy melody. This Scriptural Chaplet of Divine Mercy is based on the Penitential Psalm Scriptural Chaplet of Divine Mercy from the book, His Sorrowful Passion. Brother Leonard Konopka, MIC, prays selections from the Seven Penitential Psalms, while Nancy Scimone's crystal clear soprano voice brings us God's message of Divine Mercy

Quantity orders of Suffering Servant Scriptorium books or CDs may be purchased for liturgical, educational, or sale promotional use.
For discount schedule and further information, please write:

Special Markets Dept., Suffering Servant Scriptorium,
PO Box 1126
Springfield, VA 22151

Or call us at 888-652-9494.